The Art Of Words

THE ART OF WORDS

The Art Of Words is a spontaneous book with no chapters allowing your energy to attract any page. Including personal mantras and quotes on intuition, awareness, perspective, the mind, meditation and much more.

Adieny Nunez

©

Copyright © 2013 Adieny Nunez. All rights reserved. No part of this book may be reproduced or transmitted in any form or by any means, electronic, mechanical, photocopy, recording, digital, or any information storage and retrieval system now known or to be invented, without written permission from the publisher, except by a reviewer who may quote brief, attributed excerpts in connection with a review.

ISBN: 1522831053
ISBN 13: 9781522831051

Everyone is exactly where he or she needs to be—the present moment.

Fearing the ability to feel gives the ego more room to control your life. If you are happy, feel it. If you are sad, feel it. Do not hold emotions inside. Happiness should be expressed; sadness should be released.

When you remove what you don't need, the universe gives you everything you've always wanted. In order for something to enter, something must be given away.

Be with someone who lets you discover the world—someone who allows your soul to be free rather than to drown in fear. Fear is what keeps us trapped.

The perfect practice is always patience—to be patient with yourself and everything surrounding you.

Allow angry people to be no more than a test in your life. Instead of giving in to their anger, give in to your peace.

The ego likes to judge others in order to feel better about itself. Be aware of this and stop feeding into it.

Today I will gain patience, and I will remain consistent in everything I do and say.

Be faithful to others, but first learn to be faithful to yourself.

Your mind is a powerful tool; it must be controlled and acknowledged to better yourself and your life.

The mind plays tricks. When you think you've gained control, the mind guides you to where it wants to be. Gain self-awareness. Own what is yours. Break the cycle of negative thoughts.

The truth within our souls can never escape. Do not live a life based only on the outer world; seek inside yourself, where you'll find most of the answers.

The past is a place to which you cannot return. So why backtrack?

Some people are like bridges in our lives. We must connect with them to reach the other side. People are also lessons, and lessons come to an end. Just don't forget the experience you had crossing to the other side.

Allow your ambitions and creativity to elevate your day; do not just dwell in your thoughts. Allow all the good inside of you to keep you headed in the right direction.

Live your life the way you want to, not the way others expect you to. Most of the time we want to please others to make them happy, and we end up forgetting our own needs.

Never regret something that made you grow. Experiences are lessons that lead to blessings. At the end of the day, everything you experience is part of the journey. You must have certain experiences for personal growth.

Whether the sun is out or it is raining, whether it is Monday or Friday, maintain your motivation and happiness. By dreading the rain or Monday, your attitude radiates through your day and attracts other negatives.

When seeking to be better, gain and maintain the strength to take action. Do not rush through your process to get immediate results. After all, it's the process that makes us who we are. Do not lose motivation over time.

Do not give in to your mind when your heart says otherwise. Your mind plays tricks on you. It makes you focus on anything, whether good or bad. Focus on what the heart wants, not the mind.

Do not bury negative emotions. Feel them, and then let them go. The body does not need to accumulate pain. Release it all.

To be free is to be free from your mind because that is what traps you and makes you feel like a prisoner. When you become free from all thought, you become free from everything else.

It is easy to judge; the mind is used to judging everything, even itself. Judging negatively allows us to see how tricky the mind is. Replace judgments with compliments.

When love touches the heart, no distance can undo that touch.

Do not allow your ego to overpower your life. Know your mind; know yourself! Know that you are not controlled by your thoughts.

Open your mind to the inner visions of your soul.

Feed your strengths, not your weaknesses. Give your all to do your best. Do not pay attention to your can'ts.

If you stay connected to your awareness and your patterns, you can break any cycle that isn't positive for your life and self-growth.

There's nothing wrong with a little challenge. See it as an opportunity to grow.

The cover attracts us, but it's what is inside that changes us. Just like books and people, what's inside doesn't show on the cover.

You are a work of art, and so are the words you speak. Make them beautiful!

Treating each day the right way will make things better. What is the right way? Cherish every day to your benefit; it is yours.

When you walk, walk as if the world is your runway.
Walk as if the sun or moon is your spotlight.

Do not settle for a good kiss when you are fed bad lies.

A wise person knows when he or she is wrong. Accept it when you are wrong because the ego always wants to be right. Being right isn't a form of power or strength.

I am light, I am love, I am understanding and forgiving.

Find time to relax body, mind, and soul.

Listening is the greatest gift. Listening has become such a difficult thing for people to do. Be present in the moment, and listen when someone speaks. Do not interrupt. Listen without thinking of something to say.

Feed your faith, not your fears. Believe it or not, everyone's beliefs are based on either faith or fear. But you have the power to feed off one rather than the other.

You cannot forget what someone has done to you, but you can overcome the past and give in to forgiveness. Forgiving isn't always about someone else; it can be about you with yourself. Forgiving is a form of letting go.

Find hope in hopeless moments. You are the hope when there is none. You are the "I can" when everything seems to be "I can't."

The mind is a powerful tool. Use it wisely for your growth and happiness. After all, it's yours—something you own. Don't allow it to use you.

A thought can either build you up as a person or destroy you. Control your thoughts for a positive outcome. You are not your thoughts, but you end up attracting what you think about.

Working hard for success isn't easy, but it's much more difficult to attain success when you don't work for what you desire. The key to attracting what you want isn't only visualizing it in your mind; it's also working toward that vision.

There are no secrets to success, only tools. And all those tools are inside of you.

Never neglect the sensation of love. Life itself is love, and you are love. Embrace it!

A thought is what gets you up in the morning. As powerful as a thought is, it can change your mood or your perception of any situation.

When you are constantly in search of something or someone, you are never able to see what is in front of you.

When life gets harder, you instantly become stronger. Repeat this truth to yourself when you feel too much weight on your shoulders.

You can have new energy and new force, but nothing can happen unless you allow it to. Do not close yourself up to the greatness inside you and the gifts of the universe that await you.

Be wise and follow your imagination. No dream is too big.

We tend to attract people who are reflections of our inner selves. It takes a great deal of awareness to see and feel this force. We find ourselves in others daily; it may be the good or the bad parts of us because the chain of life presents us with a mirror of ourselves each day.

What better way to start the day than with a smile and open arms? Open your heart to the world; don't live in the fetal position. Open yourself up.

Just because you are not asleep doesn't mean you can't keep dreaming.

Just because you change your beliefs doesn't mean you didn't succeed. All it means is that you are finding new ways of making it work.

Never agree with a lie just because you don't like the truth. A lie can only last so long. Sometimes a lie seems ideal and gives hope, the hope to see change. But truth is the light in the darkness, and a lie can never be anything more than a falsehood.

Learn to let go of fear, the ego, and the past. You can learn from these three things, but none of them can be useful for you to live in. Notice what you fear and let it go. Acknowledge your ego, the identity that isn't who you really are, and let go of it. The past is only useful when one is reflecting in a positive way on one's personal growth.

You don't need to travel the world to see true beauty; all you need to do is open your eyes.

Don't turn simplicity into complexity. Truth is always simple; it's our way of understanding that makes it complicated.

Learn to give without expectations. Do things from the heart for yourself and for others. Sometimes when we do things based on expectations, they don't turn out as we think they will.

Do not constantly judge yourself; help yourself. We are our toughest critics. Be the observer to become the helper. Do not trap yourself with your own judgments.

To find inner peace, you must accept all that's around you. Inner peace is a better understanding of your inner and outer selves.

Be at peace with the good and bad while aiming for better. No matter what happens, maintain your peace while using your balance to overcome obstacles.

Never allow a bad experience to interfere with new experiences. An experience leads to a story in our minds, a story that is compared to anything similar. Allow your experiences, whether good or bad, to be. But do not limit anything in your life because of a past experience.

What is positive thinking without positive action? Change your mind to a better state and work toward those changes.

If your wishes do not arrive, go and make them true.

When all else fails, remember there is nowhere else to go but up. At the top is where you belong, and to the top is where you will be.

If you are not surrounded by positive motivators, be the motivator.

Time and experience are the greatest teachers in life.

If you cannot find a plan, don't worry; you do not need it. Keep going and growing! Life showers us with presents, and those presents are usually unexpected or even contrary to our plans.

Don't be the one to complicate yourself. Be your ultimate light in order to see clearly.

You can achieve all that you believe. If you believe you cannot, then you will stop yourself; if you believe you can, you will get there. Our beliefs affect us for the greater good or for the bad, because what you believe you tend to attract and become.

Work hard, but work toward a purpose. Your work is your purpose!

True love is loving yourself. To feel complete love with another being, you must first discover the love within.

What's knowledge without action? Act on what you know, even if it's difficult.

One way or another, we give so much of ourselves to people. What's better than to give something as positive as knowledge, compassion and love?

Love isn't about possession; love is about the fire in a slow dance between two people wanting to share the song, not two people wanting to own the song.

Do not fear the unknown, for it may be filled with blessings. To fear something that you do not know is like setting limits to your life's journey. Perhaps the unknown is familiar to your soul.

Trust in the universe and trust in yourself. It is lack of trust that brings fear and worry into your mind and into your life.

Do not allow anyone to take away your peace. Your peace cannot be taken away. No one can take you out of your own happiness.

Cherish those who are constantly there for you; never lack the willingness to show appreciation.

All the peace you need is within you. You are peace!

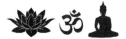

To fix a problem, you don't always need to act; sometimes you can just allow things to be. In some situations, you must act; in others, you should surrender to stillness and allow things to fall into place.

Do not run away when you are meant to stay. Have patience with the present when you wish to be "there;" and remember you are not done being "here."

Worry less about how others see you, and worry more about how you see yourself. The insane choice is focusing on the judgments of others and neglecting your own knowledge.

Always ask yourself whether your ego wants it or your heart desires it. When your awareness is under control, you will be more in tune with your decisions and where they are coming from.

Speak less about the problem, and look toward the solution. Knowing your situation allows you to fix it, but discussing it over and over again is not going to make your problem disappear. The faster you take action, the faster your problem becomes part of the past. Always maintain a clear vision of ways to make your life better instead of closing one eye and dwelling on the issue.

Enjoy nature—it's free. Try noticing the essence of nature. The flowers, how they bloom for the world, the clouds, how they come and go. The stillness of a tree and most of all the air that you breathe, take time to breathe and appreciate.

Be the observer. There is no need to judge. Self-help allows you to remove the need to judge. Fall into the world of observation not judgment.

Live your journey, and don't be afraid to enjoy it. Sometimes your happiness is another person's sadness, but by the end of the day, you cannot stop yourself from pursuing your own journey and happiness.

"Today I will practice patience; I will challenge myself, and I will succeed." Today, tomorrow, and the following day are about you. Live the life you want with those you want to live with. Be your own opponent, challenge yourself, and believe in your outcome.

If you change, do so for the better. We are constantly changing, so make sure your growth is headed in a positive direction.

Do not choose to be miserable just because it is comfortable. There is nothing wrong with wanting to be comfortable, but why choose it when you are not happy? It's an illusion. The true comfort is happiness, not the safety of something familiar.

Move forward knowing what you are leaving behind as you take the next route. Then you do not have to keep looking back while you move ahead.

Pain creates holes, and love fills those holes. Pain is inevitable, and so is love. The beauty in pain is that it is overcome by love.

Allow pain to heal properly; do not bury it inside. Take all the time you need to heal.

Laugh more. Love more. Feel more. The beauty of life is our own emotions, our laughter that brings joy and our love that brings life.

Pain is not what we live by, it's what we learn from. You are not your pain; you are what you learn through the process.

To ask is easy, but to show gratitude is easier. Do not waste another second before showing gratitude for the things in life you have received, for the lessons you have learned, and for the people you know or have met.

Meditation calms the mind; it allows you to reflect in a positive way, to clear your mind and thoughts, and to find stillness and peace. Meditation brings peace of mind to your life and allows you to find peace within yourself and your thoughts. It is a practice that helps you gain self-awareness in your daily life.

Find the balance between when to remain patient and when to be aggressive. Success requires both—but never at the same time.

If you do not like something, change it. If you cannot change it, accept it. There is the person who hates his job and complains about it without taking action. Then there is the person who dislikes his job but who accepts that it is only temporary until he finds a better position. The more you repeat certain words and scenarios, the more they will affect you and your health. If you cannot change a situation, change your outlook of what you do not like, and things will change for you. Your thoughts can change and allow you to cope with anything.

We always end up predicting what we believe, so predict things that include possibility. Find no limits in what you wish, believe in everything, and most importantly, believe in yourself.

Don't confuse closeness with clinginess. There is nothing in this world that you need to cling to. Stay close, yes, but to cling is about possession. Closeness is not about possession but about freedom.

Don't make decisions based on comfort; make decisions from the heart. Follow your heart, even if it takes you down a dark alley. Every alley has an end with light, so do not be afraid to take the walk.

Trust that the universe knows what it's doing. Trust that mistakes are lessons that lead to progress.

Think back to a time when you had a difficult situation in your life; think about how hard it was then. Now think about how you are today. Life is an endless experience in which we always overcome the difficulties no matter what they are. The past belongs in the past. The present never forsakes you.

Stress can be removed, or it can be increased. It's common for all beings to feel stress. The keys to removing stress are patience and awareness, along with your words and actions. Don't be the one to increase your own stress and live continuously in the pattern and pain it brings to the body.

Don't stay in a relationship because you don't like to be alone. The moment you feel that you need someone else to feel complete, you lose something important. The moment you feel that emptiness inside you, allow it to teach you about yourself, and know you are in need of your own self. To desire a mate is human nature, but to feel incomplete is the body screaming for peace. Be able to be alone and happy, and then you'll wind up with someone who is happy, as well. A partner meets you halfway to become whole with you; a partner does not come to be the whole of you.

During the day, take a couple of minutes for yourself and get in tune with your emotions. Sometimes we forget to look inside and quiet the mind. Connect with yourself. Nothing is more precious than the connection of hearing and feeling your own heart.

The guide is called the intuition, and the mind is called the distraction. Allow yourself to remain connected to your self-awareness, and maintain that connection with your intuition while avoiding the distractions of the mind.

No one knows you better than you know yourself. Seek inside yourself for answers. All that you need to know will always be within you. You can seek advice, but true guidance will always reside within you. Even before your mind makes a decision, your insides knew much earlier.

When you finish a relationship, it's good to take some time for yourself. Don't begin to search or jump into something just because you can't be alone. Give yourself the time you need, and allow the universe to bring someone into your life at the right moment. Time is the healer of all and the teacher of all, and taking time allows the right people to enter at the right moment.

Temptation is a part of life—this you know. Be strong enough to put any type of temptation aside. When you become aware, you see the temptation before you. Maintain your footing on your path; do not put yourself in a position to be tempted.

Every decision we make triggers some kind of fear. Fear comes with ifs or buts. Remove the fear to act and think more clearly. Do not fall into a thought that creates fear when all you need to do is change your thought.

Do not keep surrounding yourself with people who constantly drain you. Care enough about yourself to be alone, or with different people, instead of being around the wrong type of energy for you.

You cannot change most situations. In order to be happy, you need to accept your reality. You cannot change most of the situations you are in, but circumstances are not forever. When you can't change a situation, accept it for the moment. By accepting it, you will bring more happiness into your life, but first you must change your state of mind. If you want a positive change, be it; then you will see it.

A clean home is a clear home. Allow the energies to flow in the place that is also known as your temple. Your home is like your body. If you do not clean it, it will be dirty, and it will not feel good. Maintain the energies in your home as you do your body: fresh and clean. It makes a difference to your state of living and the vibes that come into your life.

What is talent without confidence? Believe in yourself, and believe in all that you have to provide to life. Do not allow your fear and lack of confidence to stop you from becoming the person you were meant to be. Believe in yourself because you will be surprised at what you can do and who you can become.

Life is like a game. The more you practice, the better you become.

Accept yourself in order to learn how to accept others. Judgments and complications begin when you are unable to be who you are and find problematic issues with everyone else. Know yourself, and love yourself. Then you'll feel love and acceptance for others.

To get to where you want to be, you must know how to handle where you are now. It's as if one cannot walk but is aiming to run. First handle today, then approach the steps you must take to reach your goal.

What is a dream without a risk? Do not fear taking a risk, because fear doesn't exist. Fear is a manmade emotion. To make your dream happen, you will have to give all of yourself. Then you can go places and have experiences you never imagined. When you feel that you can't, know that you are already halfway; once you've begun, you are halfway to the goal.

Do not fight so much that you wind up fighting yourself. Seek inner peace for release.

I will believe more in myself, I will believe more in others. I will have no expectation.

Don't hold on when you are meant to let go. We are either holding on or letting go. Know when it's time to let go.

You can either listen to your thoughts or feel and listen to your intuition. Your intuition will never fail you.

Grow your ambition and give yourself what you deserve—the very best and nothing less. This you must see and believe.

Don't allow your mind to take away your motivation. Control your thoughts!

You can move to another state or country to search for peace, but if you do not have it inside yourself, you'll always be searching for something you already have. You will capture beauty and peaceful moments in any journey, but the real peace is already within you.

Receiving blessings is a gift. From a new job to a newborn, a new friend, or a new lesson, you can name almost anything you encounter in your day, and chances are it will be filled with blessings.

Acknowledge the difference between what is wrong and what is fear.

Forgiving is a sign of strength, not weakness. Be strong enough to let go instead of holding onto grudges. The art of forgiving will surprise you in how better things are and how much better you feel after you've let go.

You didn't come into this life to suffer. Try your best to keep it that way. Pain is uncontrollable, but you can choose if you want to suffer. Suffering continues and expands the pain. Work to heal the pain and avoid suffering through your days. Always find a door to release the pain.

Remove the "I," because it represents the ego that your mind has created. Do not feed this false sense of identity that you do not need.

Do not allow pleasure to turn into an addiction that you cannot live without. There is nothing wrong with pleasure, but when it's abused, it becomes addictive. You do not need anything to depend on or cling to.

Challenge yourself in order to evolve. How will you know how far you can climb if you do not try? But it takes more than trying, it takes not giving up. To not give up is a challenge for everyone.

Remove judgment and replace it with love. It is easy to judge and find faults in others because no one is perfect. Removing the judgment allows a person to see with love and appreciation.

No matter what you do or where you go, never forget to keep loving yourself.

Some of the patterns in our lives are a reflection of who we are inside and/or hereditary cycles being repeated. Break those chains, and change yourself and your life for the better.

Remove old blockages, because neglecting them is what created them in the first place. It's all about the power of seeing then letting go.

Giving yourself a title is like putting yourself in a room and calling it living. Don't limit yourself. Live to your fullest potential. In order to see what your fullest potential is, you must see all that's inside you and take action without limits.

I have what it takes. Believe and repeat

Long to find inner peace; long to remove what you do not need. Sometimes a more peaceful state can be found after we make a few changes within ourselves.

After you decide on something, challenge yourself to achieve it. It's you against you. There are those who only know how to start, and there are others who know how to finish. When you catch yourself stopping halfway, focus and remember what motivated you to begin in the first place.

Perhaps the life you wanted wasn't the life you needed. You will always end up in the place that is best for you. Consider them man who is a musician who wanted to be famous and show the world his talents, but ended up owning a music school helping others to achieve their dreams. Instead of the musician using his instrument, life made him an instrument to impact and change the lives of others. You will be where you belong, and along the way, you will realize that what you wanted wasn't necessarily what you needed.

When you allow your ego to get in the way as pride or anger, you close all avenues leading you farther on your journey. Don't close your avenues!

Lying only leads to more lying, and that's not living. Anything you do becomes a pattern. Love leads to more love, hatred leads to more hatred, peace leads to more peace. Create your own path, and let it be a path that will bring good to you and those around you.

Make time to be thankful for all you have and how far you've come.

I will never lose hope, I will ever lose faith, I will never stop believing.

The mind has questions, the soul has answers.

To live in the mind is to take a detour from life.

The past will never come back; the past is a still place. Leave the past where it belongs: behind.

Life is lived when one is fully awake in the present moment. Being awake doesn't mean to have your eyes open. It means giving in to the now.

No end can kill you unless it's the end of your life. Lift yourself up!

If laziness is stopping you from doing something great, remember that laziness means failure. It's always great to find ways to motivate and lift yourself up.

Long to be in a place that you call faith. Long to take hold of the strength that you already own.

Do not trap a person who needs or wants to be free, including yourself.

Words have such a strong power over our lives. Use your words wisely.

Change your perspective, change your life.

It did not last for a reason. Bury the past.

Who you were means nothing compared to who you've become. Forget the old you and embrace the person you are today.

Big moves require big risks. If you wish to aim high, be willing to jump high.

Fighting for love is worth it when the other person is fighting with you, not against you.

Life has many levels of progress, the higher, the better.

Love tenderly. Love purely. Love whenever. Love forever.

Which way should you go? Follow your instincts not your ego.

Don't stay stuck in past relationships; be open to a new and better love. Be open to a new beginning without judgments. Seeking the past will only provide an illusion of what was and prevent what is about to come.

Do not create expectations for others; create them for yourself!

Respect your mother's and father's energies. Do not judge them, for they brought you to life. Love and accept them the way they are.

Nothing is permanent; do not fear a problem because it will not last.

Seeking perfection is to neglect all.

Not everyone lives in the same reality, not everyone has to. Instead of focusing on getting people to love and understand you, attract people into your same frequency.

New love should never be compared to old love; appreciate the good instead of seeking what you used to have. What you had is now in the past; allow who is in your present a proper chance to stay.

Never punish someone for your mistakes. To make a mistake is punishment enough, but to punish someone else for your wrongs is far worse.

Deep within, you will always have the answers. The outer world is where you find all your precious questions.

Value yourself so you do not hurt yourself. Try to avoid putting yourself in a position that will hurt you even before you begin.

Never give up on what you love just to give in to confusion.

Honesty is a good value to live by. Maintain honesty with yourself and others. Honesty always avoids confusion and the circus ring of drama.

Gain the courage to stand up for what matters to you. Never be afraid to fight for what you believe in.

Love is not infatuation; love is freedom.

Material things reflect only your outer life. People want them but do not need them.

Worrying about how people see you or think of you will be a worry you'll have forever. Do yourself a favor and pay no attention to the perceptions of others. You know your truths.

Always be a helping hand.

Close the door to negativity, and open the door to light and purity. Allow these things to brighten your life and the lives of those around you.

If you cannot be at ease with yourself, how can you be completely and genuinely at ease with others? Either you will become purely at ease with yourself, or you'll become dependent on someone else to make you at ease with yourself. And to depend on others for happiness is like closing your eyes to life.

Most people create an image of how they think they are supposed to be. Your being is developed over time; allow yourself to grow naturally instead of forcing yourself to become someone you are not and perhaps do not want to be. Growth cannot be planned. It's what you learn and who you become through life's lessons.

We must take action to get what we want, not just make requests.

The beauty of life is that no matter what happens, it will always work out.

Seek inside for the missing key; seek outside for the door. There is nothing like two well-connected worlds.

Remain gracefully patient.

We all seek the answers to questions when we are the ultimate answer.

Do not allow your lack of confidence to push you to the side when you were meant to stand in the center. Be confident in your ability to stand out.

Fall in love with the eyes it'll never lie.

We are all teachers, but we must learn how to become students in order to teach.

Do not look so far into the future that you live in anxiety while trying to reach it. Live for today; be present and slow it down.

Running elsewhere to find yourself is a race you cannot win. You must seek within. It's impossible to run from yourself.

Do not fear being alone. Solitude will bring you the ultimate peace.

Do not allow the mind or the ego to define the way you are. See yourself as you are, not as the mind portrays you to be.

Life starts when you release all that is inside you.

Today, I will no longer listen to my mind. Today, I will let go and gain control.

Take care of your body; no one else will.

We are all our own therapists. The problem is that we are deaf to our own voices. Listen, because you always have what you need to know.

Feed the soul what it needs.

Chasing after what hurts you and ignoring something that is good for you shows a lack of self-awareness.

Most situations are not as complex as your mind perceives them to be. See every situation as having a solution if you wish to make your life easier—and who wouldn't want that?

Energy flows through the body; allow that energy to flow. Don't create blockages, because every blockage keeps the energy stuck.

Shower before you go to bed to have the best sleep; let the energy of your day wash away.

Tears are a powerful form of therapy; let them out if you need to.

Letting go doesn't mean only physically, it also means mentally and emotionally.

Gain self-awareness to know if something or someone is a positive attraction or simply a distraction.

Believe in yourself and believe in your path, even if it takes some unexpected turns.

Begin each day in a positive state of mind. You have all the tools to proceed, mentally, emotionally, and physically.

Ask yourself an important question when you are fulfilling a desire: Is it your ego's desire or your soul's?

Listen to your intuition and follow what you feel. If you can't distinguish between your mind and your intuition, practice being in tune with yourself on a daily basis. Meditation helps!

When you know yourself, it's easy to make decisions.

Listen to your thoughts and watch yourself. In order to learn and change, you must start by listening and observing.

Become aware of what you do; your actions define who you are.

Do not wait until you lose something to begin to value it.

Feel the pure sensation of love; allow it to flow like energy, naturally.

You have the power to manifest ANYTHING. Believe it and you will see it

Embrace your soul's desire, and do not be afraid.

If you choose to be comfortable, be comfortably at peace.

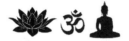

No one can force you to do something you do not want to do. Make decisions based on what you want, not what others think.

Marriage is a commitment between two, not three or more.

If you choose to dwell on something, dwell on progress, not sadness.

The repetition of mistakes is a chain you are meant to break. Change your life for the better, even if it means letting go of the past. After all, you belong in the now.

Don't fight with the mind, because the conflict will only get worse. Remove insignificant thoughts or you'll wind up amplifying them.

To know what is wrong yet continue to do it is to show a lack of self-control.

To feel empty is to satisfy the ego, for the heart is meant to be fulfilled.

Life never goes back, only the mind does.

Breathe more; think less.

Never take a loved one for granted.

Believe in something, but mainly believe in yourself.

Gain awareness to stop your moods from swinging.

The Art Of Words

Being a person of your word means being honest with yourself.

Express what you feel, because emotions must be freely open. Closing yourself only allows your shield to grow stronger, making it harder for anyone to reach in.

Somewhere down the line you picked a life of passion or principle. Imagine creating a life with both.

You cannot escape time; you can only accept it.

Love is beautiful; feel it and embrace it.

Why shine with someone else's light when you have your own?

Self-expression is hard, especially when you have been hurt before, but pain is one of life's most powerful forms of learning.

Awareness allows you to see the problem and find a solution. While the mind is ready to react to everything, take a second to observe.

See others with love, not negative judgment.

Bring out the talents you have within, and believe in those talents. Don't allow false thoughts lead to insecurity. Be confident!

To repeat a mistake is a part of life, but do not forget the lesson and wind up reliving your mistake.

Time after time, we aim for the unthinkable, hoping it will be what our minds expect. Aim with your heart because it knows best.

Focus on what is coming, not on what has left.

The ego sees life as a game. If you think you're playing, it's playing you.

Your adulthood is a reflection of your childhood. You cannot bring your childhood back in order to fix it, but you can accept it and live today fully.

Parents affect their children. In reaction to their parents' pain, children create shields so as not to feel pain. But these shields also block joy. Feel your pain so your children do not have to.

Imperfections are not to be constantly judged, for the ego is the face of judgment.

No one can change your destiny, so do not fear the process. Destiny is already awaiting your arrival.

Do not be afraid to start over; life is about new beginnings.

The ego enjoys suffering and wants.

Allow yourself to be in the present; do not live your life in a time that's not the now.

Some choose to live in sadness, while others live to avoid it. Live to overcome sadness and achieve peace.

Anything can be simplified as "easier said than done," but all that matters is that which is attainable through hard work.

When you possess the desire to start something, you will do the unthinkable to reach it. Do not allow fear to keep you from trying.

When one loves, one shouldn't aim to be right; instead, one should aim to be in the middle in order to compromise.

Being able to control your emotions is a powerful form of knowledge and strength. Learn this control and maintain it without stuffing your emotions.

Give away what isn't yours, and give in to what you deserve.

When the heart is ready to forgive, do not allow the mind to hold on.

Don't allow your mind to keep you from finishing what you started.

Sometimes the guidance we seek is the guidance we possess: our intuition.

Be who you are, no matter what anyone says, because pleasing someone else is not worth losing yourself.

creative release helps remove the pain underneath.

Remove all of your complications and make sure you are not part of the problem.

Do not focus on how bad things are, but plan for how much better they can become.

Do not judge people by their mistakes.

Most relationships are meant to teach, not to keep. Learn and let go.

Once you've gone halfway, finish—unless it's the wrong way. Don't be afraid to adjust the course.

Be honest with others but most importantly, be honest with yourself.

When your goal feels unreachable, remember why you made it your goal. Don't stop believing!

Don't allow a few failures stop you. After all, the failures are what help you learn.

Face fear, Dominate it. Don't allow it to control you.

Do not allow a lack of confidence to stop you from reaching challenging goals.

Receive life's messages whether they come from pain or happiness.

Give up your fears and give in to faith. Believe more!

Drink what you like, not what others offer. Be your own person and make your own decisions.

Appreciate the fact that you are given a new day every day.

You are the ultimate light. Shine on!

The mind is a disorganized file; put it in order. For years your mind has produced thought after thought, whether good or bad. It's good to have mental balance and not allow your mind to generate endless thoughts.

Believe in all that you put your energy into. Even if your task seems difficult, trust and believe without negativity.

Sometimes all one needs is silence.

Feel love in the heart, not the mind.

The ego cannot experience pure love; it can only experience obsession.

Find the center within you; find the center in life.

Appreciate all that's around you. Life is not something that should be taken for granted.

Do not conform to the negativities of others.

If you want to help other people, tell them what they need to hear, not what they want to hear.

Accept that your age will change, but keep your soul young.

Be your own opponent; challenge yourself to do better.

Keep the memories that make you smile, not the ones that make you frown.

Through pain, you find joy; pain is what teaches you and allows you to grow stronger.

Connect with yourself spiritually for true peace and enlightenment.

No need to envy anyone, no need to judge and criticize. Live your own life.

Gain enough awareness to become the watcher of your every thought and action.

Know that life brings good and bad weather; know that you can find balance and happiness through it all.

It's easy to give advice and hard to follow it. Learn from your own advice.

Change from within so those around you can be inspired to make changes.

It's never too late to change, to love or take action.

When something is over, let it go. Do not go back to something you once wanted out of.

Don't change your address to a place that isn't in the present moment. There is nothing wrong with wanting what the future has to offer, but do not shift your awareness so far into the future that you escape the now. The present moment is a place that can be escaped only through the mind. Once the mind is there, it's hard to be here.

Love your children, for that love is what will nourish them. Kids need the warmth of their parents.

Just because you cannot see the sun doesn't mean it's not there.

Understand, even if you disagree.

In a relationship, do not allow the ego to interfere. Pure love does not need to cling to or convey fear.

To be emotionally numb is to neglect many wonderful things that life has for you to feel. Bad experiences are lessons that teach us to let go, not hold on.

THE ART OF WORDS

A dysfunctional person will repeat the same mistakes and attract more of the same. Break the cycle!

You can be lying on a beach, but if you do not have control of your mind, you cannot fully relax.

Be humble.

Help yourself by learning about yourself.

Do not wait for something bad or good to happen to give thanks for all your blessings.

The mind shouldn't race all the time. Regulate it.

Why neglect what you can genuinely accept?

Connect more, love more, and listen more. Be more in the present moment.

Just because you've yet to end up where you want to go, it doesn't mean you don't belong there. It only means that it's taking some time.

Words can burn like fire. Be careful what you say in the heat of passion.

Follow your dreams, not your illusions.

Success doesn't happen overnight; it happens through sweat and tears.

Don't worry too much about "what if" because things that need to happen will eventually happen. Focus on what is. What "is" is what you have, so use it. "What if" is a million things that may or may not happen. Stay focused on the "what is," and you'll be glad you neglected all those "what ifs."

When you feel like there is no hope, create your own.

Do not block out pain; blocking out pain is like keeping those emotions in storage. They need to be cleared out!

Embrace yourself and allow your light to shine and brighten up your life.

You are a success—attract what you are.

Always trust the eyes, never the words.

Love does not close your eyes. Pure love consistently works on keeping them open.

If you wish to stop, stop. You control your own life.

Break fear. Don't allow it to interfere!

You can do anything. The question is, are you willing to?

Lift yourself up instead of waiting for something or someone to do it for you.

Keep your feet on the ground while you reach for the clouds.

If there is something you cannot change, why not make the best of it? The day of the week cannot be changed, but you can change your perspective on it.

Breathe in deeply and be in the now. The breath is the stillness of your awareness.

Enjoy silence, for silence is a great form of tranquility.

Life gets better and better, harder but better.

Accept people the way they are.

A healthy relationship with the mind means letting go and creating a healthy relationship with yourself.

The Art Of Words

The first few falls are hard, but everything gets easier with time and experience.

Enjoy the sweetness of life and learn from the bitterness.

Do not define yourself upon your past experience. Who are you now?

You cannot change your parents to be the way you wish them to be. Accept the way they are, and live your life now.

If you care about everyone's opinion, you eliminate your own happiness.

The state of inner peace is achieved through stillness, patience, and understanding.

The Art Of Words

Why be rude and ruin another person's mood? Be kind!

The ego cannot survive in silence. It avoids the stillness that allows one to reach enlightenment.

The universe is always working for you, believe it and work with that energy.

The moon, as well as the sun, rises for you. Night and day are the gifts of life.

A life without love is like a person with no heart.

Choose a life that will make you happy. Whether it's hard or easy, let it make you happy, and be at peace. The source of life, freedom, inner peace, love, and happiness is you. You can be anywhere you wish, but allow that place to be as you truly want it to be.

Made in the USA
Charleston, SC
16 April 2016